EARTH'S OCEANS

AMY AUSTEN

PowerKiDS
press.

NEW YORK

Published in 2017 by The Rosen Publishing Group, Inc.
29 East 21st Street, New York, NY 10010

Editor: Caitie McAneney
Book design: Michael Flynn
Interior layout: Reann Nye

Photo Credits: Cover, p. 19 Volodymyr Goinyk/Shutterstock.com; p. 4 MB Photography/Moment/Getty Images; p. 5 Maxger/Shutterstock.com; pp. 7, 11, 13 (background) Ase/Shutterstock.com; p. 8 Brian Kinney/Shutterstock.com; p. 9 JC Photo/Shutterstock.com; p. 10 Jason LaVeris/FilmMagic/Getty Images; p. 11 Iconic Bestiary/Shutterstock.com; p. 12 Robert Hoetink/Shutterstock.com; p. 13 Designua/Shutterstock.com; p. 15 NYPL/Science Source/Getty Images; p. 16 Tomas Pavelka/Shutterstock.com; p. 17 Peter Chadwick/Gallo Images/Getty Images; p. 20 Signature Message/ Shutterstock.com; p. 21 Willyam Bradberry/Shutterstock.com; p. 22 Dudarev Mikhail/Shutterstock.com.

Cataloging-in-Publication Data

Names: Austen, Amy.
Title: Earth's oceans / Amy Austen.
Description: New York : PowerKids Press, 2017. | Series: Spotlight on earth science | Includes index.
Identifiers: ISBN 9781499425017 (pbk.) | ISBN 9781499425048 (library bound) | ISBN 9781499425024 (6 pack)
Subjects: LCSH: Ocean--Juvenile literature.
Classification: LCC GC21.5 A97 2017 | DDC 551.46--d23

Manufactured in China

CPSIA Compliance Information: Batch #BW17PK For further information contact Rosen Publishing, New York, New York at 1-800-237-9932.

CONTENTS

CHAPTER ONE

UNEXPLORED OCEANS

Have you ever been to an ocean? Oceans cover more than 70 percent of Earth's surface. They are one of Earth's most **prominent** features. For thousands of years, people have tried to unlock the mysteries of Earth's oceans.

There are still many things we don't understand about the oceans today. In fact, we've only scratched the surface! People have explored only about 5 percent of the oceans. Scientists who study the oceans are called oceanographers. They work hard each day to uncover as much as possible about these deep, blue waters.

Oceanographers have a lot of work to do to learn more about the remaining 95 percent of Earth's oceans.

There are five oceans on Earth, and they're all connected to each other. The largest ocean in the world is the Pacific Ocean. The second-largest ocean is the Atlantic Ocean. The other oceans are the Indian Ocean, Arctic Ocean, and Southern Ocean. The Southern Ocean wasn't officially called an ocean until 2000, and some people still don't recognize it as one.

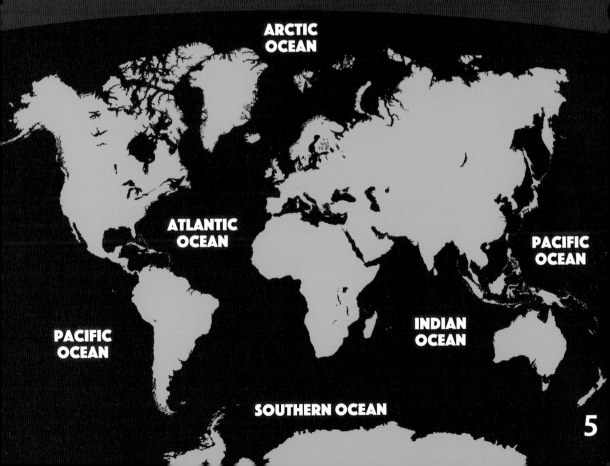

ARCTIC OCEAN

ATLANTIC OCEAN

PACIFIC OCEAN

PACIFIC OCEAN

INDIAN OCEAN

SOUTHERN OCEAN

CHAPTER TWO

FIVE OCEAN ZONES

Oceans are split into five layers depending on how deep the water is. As you go deeper into an ocean, it gets darker and colder. Pressure increases because of the weight of the water above you.

The part of an ocean that most people are familiar with is the surface layer. It's called the epipelagic zone. It's also called the sunlight zone because it receives the most light and, therefore, the most heat. Underneath this zone is the mesopelagic zone, which is also called the twilight zone. Only a little sunlight reaches this zone.

The next zone is the bathypelagic zone, which is completely dark. It's also called the midnight zone. The two deepest zones are the abyssopelagic and hadalpelagic zones. They are dark and cold, and almost nothing can exist there!

OCEAN ZONES

200 M	EPIPELAGIC ZONE (THE SUNLIGHT ZONE)	660 FT
1,000 M	MESOPELAGIC ZONE (THE TWILIGHT ZONE)	3,300 FT
2,000 M		6,600 FT
3,000 M	BATHYPELAGIC ZONE (THE MIDNIGHT ZONE)	9,900 FT
4,000 M		13,100 FT
5,000 M	ABYSSOPELAGIC ZONE (THE ABYSS)	16,300 FT
6,000 M		19,700 FT
7,000 M		23,000 FT
8,000 M		26,300 FT
9,000 M	HADALPELAGIC ZONE (THE TRENCHES)	29,600 FT
10,000 M		32,800 FT
11,000 M		36,100 FT

This diagram shows the different ocean zones. You can see that they get darker the deeper they are.

CHAPTER THREE

CORAL REEFS

Coral reefs are special ocean habitats. There aren't many coral reefs in the world, and they aren't very big compared to the size of the oceans. However, nearly 25 percent of all ocean creatures call a coral reef home.

Coral structures are made up of tiny animals called polyps. Polyps have an opening at one end that acts as a mouth. They also have **tentacles** that help them catch food. Polyps eat other tiny ocean creatures, such as algae.

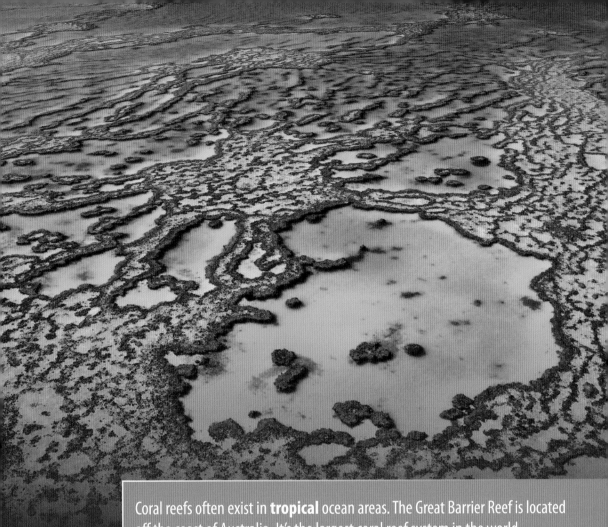

Coral reefs often exist in **tropical** ocean areas. The Great Barrier Reef is located off the coast of Australia. It's the largest coral reef system in the world.

Coral polyps often live in groups of thousands in what's called a coral colony. Over time, they create an **exoskeleton**. These skeletons form the reef structure. A coral reef is a very colorful place because of all the different kinds of coral. Fish and other marine animals love to live in coral reefs because they can hide and hunt there.

CHAPTER FOUR

THE DEEPEST OCEAN

The deep sea is an area of Earth that isn't well explored. Fewer animals exist as you go deeper. A species, or kind, of deep-sea snailfish lives deeper in the ocean than any other creature yet found. It lives more than 5 miles (8 km) underwater.

Deep-sea explorer and filmmaker James Cameron stands in front of the *Deepsea Challenger*. This vehicle took him to the deepest part of the ocean—the Challenger Deep.

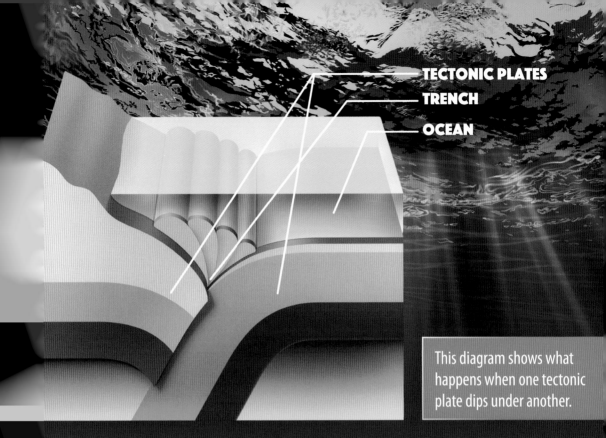

TECTONIC PLATES
TRENCH
OCEAN

This diagram shows what happens when one tectonic plate dips under another.

The deepest part of Earth's oceans is located in the Mariana Trench. This landform is located in the Pacific Ocean, east of the Philippines. A trench is a deep, narrow hole in the ocean floor. Trenches happen when **tectonic plates** collide and one plate is pushed under the other.

The Mariana Trench is more than 1,500 miles (2,414 km) long. From the ocean's surface to the trench's deepest point, it's almost 7 miles (11.3 km) deep. The deepest point is called the Challenger Deep. It's completely dark down there with

CHAPTER FIVE

MOUNTAINS AND VOLCANOES

Do you know the longest mountain range in the world is actually underwater? The mid-ocean ridge system is a mountain range that's more than 40,300 miles (64,856.6 km) long. Most of this mountain range is underwater, but about 10 percent rises above the ocean's surface.

The largest part of the mid-ocean ridge system that's above the ocean's surface is the island of Iceland. That's why Iceland has so many volcanoes and mountains.

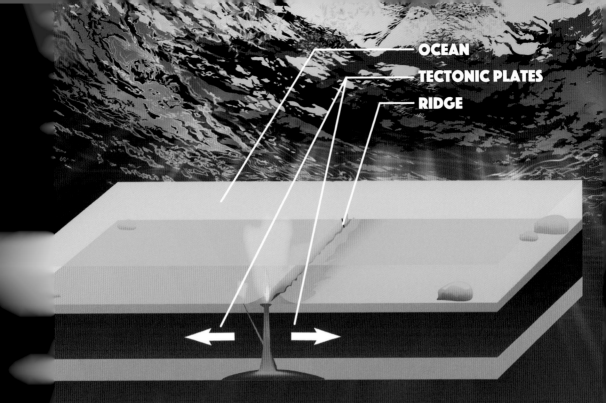

OCEAN

TECTONIC PLATES

RIDGE

Underwater mountains, or submarine mountains, occur where two tectonic plates meet, just like trenches. However, mountains form when two plates move away from each other. As they part, **molten** rock underneath the surface rises to create new land. A submarine mountain range has both peaks, or high points, and valleys, or low points.

The oceans are also home to many submarine volcanoes. Some oceanographers think there are more than 1 million underwater volcanoes. When they erupt, lava explodes into the ocean, forming new rocks along the ocean floor. Since most submarine volcanoes exist far under the water's surface, people often don't know when they erupt.

CHAPTER SIX

TSUNAMIS

Earthquakes happen when tectonic plates slip past one another. The boundary between two plates is called a fault line. There are many fault lines on land and even more in the ocean. When the plates suddenly slip by each other, they release waves of energy. When you're on land, this feels like the earth is rumbling or shaking. When it happens underwater, it can cause a tsunami.

A tsunami is very high wave, and it sometimes occurs as part of a **series** of large ocean waves. Tsunamis are caused by earthquakes, volcanic eruptions, and other major **disturbances** on the seafloor. This activity creates energy, which causes huge waves.

When a tsunami happens in the middle of an ocean, people usually don't notice. However, when it happens near a coast, people living on land may be affected. Large tsunamis can overtake streets, highways, and buildings along the coast.

Tsunamis can be huge natural disasters. Authorities estimate that up to 300,000 people were killed because of a tsunami that occurred in the Indian Ocean in 2004. These satellite photographs were taken of Sumatra, Indonesia, before and after the tsunami.

BEFORE

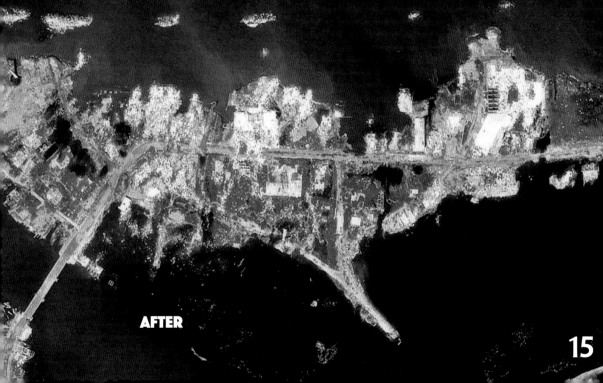

AFTER

15

CHAPTER SEVEN

TIDES AND CURRENTS

Water is always moving. Moving water is called a current. One of the causes of ocean currents is wind. You may notice that there are more waves on a windy day. That's because wind creates ocean currents on or near the surface of the water.

Tides also cause currents. Ocean tides are the rising and falling motion of water throughout the day. At high tide, the water rises and rushes over the shoreline. At low tide, the water lowers and rushes back to the sea. Tides occur because of gravity. The gravity of the sun and moon pull on Earth's oceans and create the rise and fall in water levels.

Some currents can be strong and even deadly. Rip currents, also called rip tides, happen as water flows from the shore back to the open ocean. If an obstacle is in the way, the water flows around it, creating a strong current.

STRONG CURRENTS

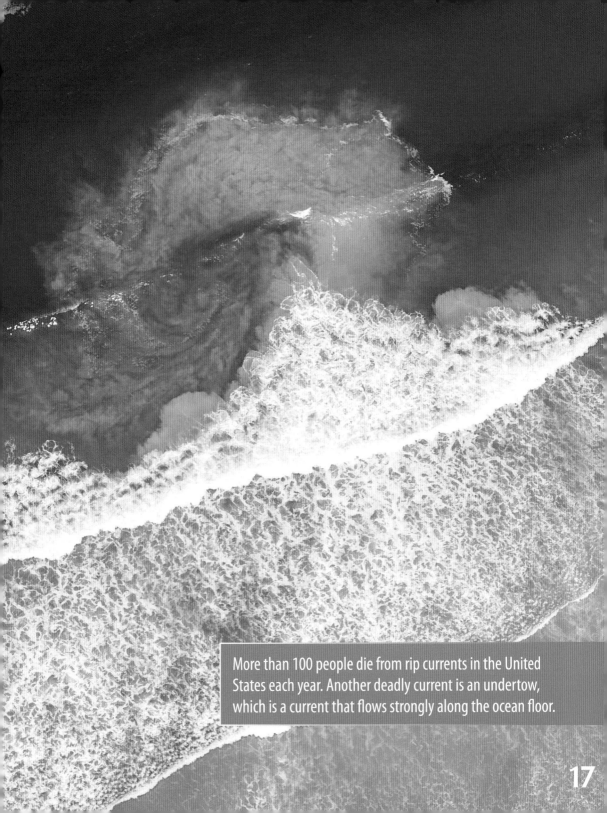

More than 100 people die from rip currents in the United States each year. Another deadly current is an undertow, which is a current that flows strongly along the ocean floor.

CHAPTER EIGHT

ECOSYSTEMS AND HABITATS

Oceans are homes to many species of plants and animals. Different zones of the ocean have different species that can live there. Some ocean habitats are warm while others are cold. Some are very salty, while others aren't as salty.

Oceans hold a great variety of ecosystems. Ecosystems are communities of living and nonliving things that interact with one another.

Coral reefs are home to thousands of species of colorful fish that feed on smaller fish and **plankton**. Blue tangs and clown fish are two kinds of fish that live in coral reefs. Deep-sea ecosystems have fewer species, but those that do live there have **adapted** to the dark and cold. Anglerfish are a good example of deep-sea fish. They have a body part that looks like a fishing rod with a light attached. It attracts smaller fish for them to eat.

ANGLERFISH

Arctic marine ecosystems are full of animals that can stand the cold! Seals, walruses, and whales that live in the Arctic Ocean have a thick layer of fat called blubber to keep them warm.

CHAPTER NINE

OCEAN ISSUES

The world's oceans are so huge that it probably seems like there's nothing humans can do to harm them. Unfortunately, that's not the case. Many ocean areas have been ruined by human pollution and **global warming**.

People dump much of their trash and waste into the water. Marine animals can die if they eat plastic bags, bottles, or foam packaging. In the northern Pacific Ocean, there's an area known as the Pacific Trash Vortex that's about the size of Texas. It's a swirling bunch of trash. Chemicals that are

Noise pollution harms ocean ecosystems, too. Sound travels far underwater and can confuse or scare migrating ocean animals.

used in farming also pollute the water. They can create dead zones, which are places where little to no ocean life can survive.

People have also burned a lot of **fossil fuels**, especially over the last 100 years. Scientists believe this has caused global warming, which is causing ocean levels to rise.

CHAPTER TEN

MYSTERIES OF THE OCEAN

Some ocean mysteries may never be solved. Why have ships disappeared in the Bermuda Triangle? Do ancient cities exist on the ocean floor? What kinds of animals live in the deep, deep sea?

However, oceanographers are hard at work exploring our oceans. As technology advances, we're able to see more of the oceans than ever before. Scientists explore the oceans using unmanned underwater vehicles, or UUVs, designed by engineers. These robots are controlled by remote or programmed to do their job. Human-operated vehicles, or HOVs, like the *Deepsea Challenger* can carry people into the deep sea. Sonar technology can map the ocean floor using a series of waves that bounce back once they hit something.

We're learning more about oceans every day. It may never be possible to explore each part of the five oceans, but we're getting closer!

GLOSSARY

adapt (uh-DAHPT) To change in order to live better in a certain environment.

disturbance (dihs-TUR-behns) A thing that upsets the natural balance in an environment.

exoskeleton (EHK-zoh-skeh-luh-tehn) The hard outer covering of an animal's body.

fossil fuel (FAH-suhl FYOOL) A fuel—such as coal, oil, or natural gas—that is formed in the earth from dead plants or animals.

global warming (GLO-buhl WAR-ming) The increase in the world's temperature that's believed to be caused by human actions.

molten (MOHL-tehn) Changed into a liquid by heat; melted.

plankton (PLANK-tehn) A tiny plant or animal that floats in the ocean.

prominent (PRAH-muh-nent) Easily noticed or seen.

series (SEE-rees) A set of things that happen one after another.

tectonic plate (tehk-TAH-nihk PLAYT) One of the moveable masses of rock that create Earth's surface.

tentacle (TEHN-tuh-kuhl) A long, thin body part that sticks out from an animal's body.

tropical (TRAH-pih-kuhl) Having to do with the warm parts of Earth near the equator.

INDEX

PRIMARY SOURCE LIST

Page 10
Deepsea Challenger shown with James Cameron. Photograph. Created by Jason LaVeris at California Science Center in Los Angeles, California. 2013. Getty Images.

Page 15
An overhead view of Sumatra, Indonesia, before and after the earthquake and tsunami of December 26, 2004. Satellite images. 2004.

Page 18
Deep-sea anglerfish. Specimen found by Natural Energy Lab of Hawaii Authority, Keahole, Kona, Hawaii. Photograph by Doug Perrine. Getty Images.

WEBSITES

Due to the changing nature of Internet links, PowerKids Press has developed an online list of websites related to the subject of this book. This site is updated regularly. Please use this link to access the list: www.powerkidslinks.com/soes/ocean